For
Billy and Poppy
and Em x
M H

For Joseph and Gabriel
with all my love
N D

this BOOK
belongs to:
- - - - - - - - - - -

Nicola Davies

OUTSIDE your WINDOW

A FIRST BOOK of NATURE

illustrated by

Mark Hearld

Candlewick Press

Contents

Spring

Summer

Autumn

Winter

Spring

Spring is the busiest season. Plants and animals are waking up after their winter rest, and there's so much to do—flowers to grow, eggs to lay, babies to feed! Everywhere you look there's something happening.

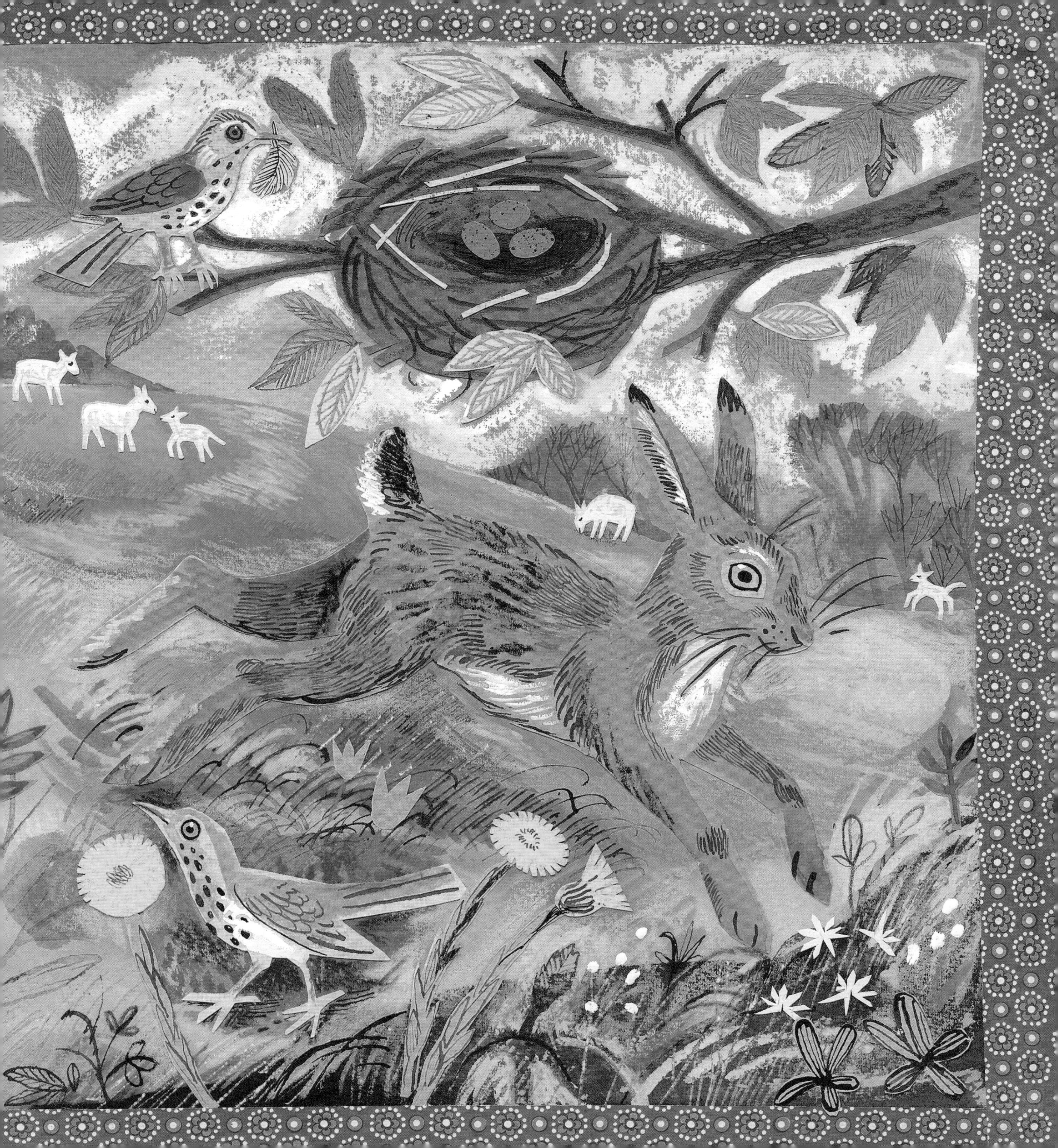

Water

The icicles melt,
and water whispers:
Drip! Drip! Drip!

The stream flows,
and water chatters:
Gurgle! Gurgle! Gurgle!

The rain falls on the grass,
and water sings:
Grow! Grow! Grow!

Bulbs

Look! Look! There's a green shoot in the snow!
A bulb is sprouting.
The cold still bites and the wind still blows,
but something tells the bulb that it's time to grow.
Inside its brown coat and layers like an onion,
a tiny pulse beats,
counting out the days like a calendar,
so the bulb knows winter's almost gone
and soon it will be time for leaves and flowers.

Listen to the Pond

Listen! Can you hear it?

Rrrrruurrrrp. Rrrrrruuurp. Rrrrrruuup.

The frogs are croaking in the pond

and laying eggs like spotted jelly.

Next week the spots will be wiggly tadpoles.

Next month they'll grow a pair of legs.

By summer they'll be tiny frogs that leap off into the world.

And one night in another spring, when they're big frogs,

they'll be back!

Rrrrruurrrrp. Rrrrrruuurp. Rrrrrruuup.

Catkin Song

All along the winding river,
in the hedges by the lane,
on the wasteland by the factory,
spring is coming once again.

Dancing, golden yellow catkins,
pussy willows' silvery shine,
side by side on twigs and branches,
showing winter's had its time.

12

Dandelions

Dandelions bloom like little suns.

But the flowers don't last long—

they fold up like furled umbrellas pointing at the sky.

Then each rolled umbrella opens

into a puff of down:

a hundred fluffy parachutes, each carrying a small brown seed.

Just one blow and you can set them flying.

Migration

In the treetops, in the bushes,

there are new songs and colors.

The little birds are back!

They've flown so far!

Over forests, mountains, deserts, seas—

such a long, long way to get back to us.

Yet here they are,

bright and alive, fluttering, singing,

ready for spring.

Gull Flight

Flap-flap-flap, flap-flap-flap!

The gull runs into the wind,

wings working hard for takeoff.

Flaap! Flaap!
It scoops the air with big, long strokes
and climbs into the sky.

Soar!
It holds its wings straight and still
to ride the warm air, up, up, up!

Glide!
Now it bends them to make a *W*
and slides down the wind
toward the sea.

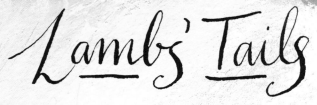

Lambs' Tails

Lambs' tails wiggle when they're happy—
a wiggle, wiggle, squiggle
that shows just how they feel.

You'll see it happen when a lamb is feeding.
It butts its mom and starts to suck,
then watch its tail go!

All over the fields in spring,
lambs' tails are wiggling.
When you see them, you just want to smile.

Nesting

The birds are busy nest building,

dashing back and forth—

first with twigs and grasses to make the nest cup,

then with wisps of fluff and tiny feathers

to make a soft, cozy lining

that will keep their eggs all safe and warm.

Cherry Blossoms

Last week the twigs were just twigs,
bare and black and boring,
but now—blossoms!

At first there were only little patches
of pink petals,
but now—blossoms, blossoms!

In parks, on streets, in gardens—
pools of pink spread,
and now we're lost in blossoms, blossoms, blossoms!

Rainbows

When the sun shines through the rain,
watch out for rainbows!

Sunlight's made of colors—
red, orange, yellow, green, blue, indigo, violet—
all mixed together.

But when sunlight shines through rain,
the raindrops can unmix the colors.
Then . . . watch out for rainbows!

Planting Seeds

Seeds are so small!

So hard and dry,

like fingernails or grains of sand.

How can they grow into something you can eat?

With your help, they can!

Plant them in some soil,

crumbly and moist as cake mix.

Not too deep and not too shallow.

Then water them. . . . Then wait.

Under the earth,

the seeds soak up water, swell, and come to life.

When you see the shoots of green,

you know your seeds aren't seeds anymore,

but baby carrots, squash, corn, and cabbage.

Your tiny seeds have grown into things

that soon you'll want to eat!

Veggie peelings
Apple cores
Dead Leaves
and Flowers
Shreds of paper
Banana skins
the Hair Mom
cut off your
BANGS

Making Compost

Peelings from the kitchen,
cuttings from the garden.
Inside the compost bin
they wilt and wither and then rot.
Slowly, over months and months,
they change and turn brown and crumbly . . . compost!
Spread it on the garden to help plants grow.

Summer

Lazy summer, warm and sweet.

Long, long days full of bees and flowers.

Time to dip your toes in the sea or watch

the breeze moving through the grass.

Time to pick a ripe tomato right off

the plant and pop it in your mouth.

Time to look at the sky

and dream.

Summer Song

In the city park at sunrise,

a little brown bird sings,

"Tu-loo, tu-loo, tu-loo,

chuck, chuck, weeeeeeeee!"

His song says, "This tree is mine!"

At midday in the hot, dry grass,

a cricket rubs a leg along his wing.

"Chirr chirr, chirr chirr, chirr chirr!"

His song says, "Come and be my mate!"

32

In the pond at midnight,

the frog's throat puffs up to

call, "Rrrruuup, rrrruuup,

rrruuup, rrruuuuup!"

His song says, "I'm the biggest!"

Everywhere you go, just listen:

someone's always singing.

Flowers

Without a sound the flowers call out.

They shout to insects with their colors—

yellow, red and orange,

blue and pink and white:

"Come here! Come here!

Right here is where

you'll find the nectar."

Honey

Buzzzzzzz zzzzzzz . . .

It's coming from the beehive.
It sounds like sweetness
and the sleepy, sleepy summer.

Hummm mmm . . .

The bees bring nectar from the flowers
for miles around, and in the hive,
they make it into honey.

Buzzzzz zzzzz . . .

Hummmmmmmm mmmmmm . . .

The sound of sweetness and the smell of flowers,
of sunny, sleepy summer—
the sound of honey.

Baby Birds

Are there baby birds inside the nest yet?

Creep close and listen.

Can you hear tiny little voices calling out?

It's the chicks, with their beaks wide open,

saying, "Feed me, feed me,

feed me."

Making Hay

The meadow, full of sunshine,
warm grass, and flowers,
has been cut for hay,
swirled up into big round bales.

They'll be stacked inside the barn now,
high as the roof,
storing summer's goodness
for the cows to eat when winter comes.

Milking

Slowly, slowly down the path,
the cows come to be milked.
Underneath, their udders swing,
full and heavy, hard to carry.

Afterward, back in the meadow,
the cows graze in the sun.
All day eating, all day chewing,
making milk from grass again.

Caterpillars, Butterflies

What's eating the leaves,

making them like lace and rags?

Caterpillars!

Caterpillars!

It's all they do,

eat leaves and grow and grow....

And when they've finished growing,

they make a bag

that's called a chrysalis

and go to sleep inside it.

Inside,

the caterpillar

changes to a butterfly.

If you don't believe it, look!

A chrysalis

is splitting open. . . .

You can watch

the wings unfolding in the sunshine.

A butterfly.

Pond Dipping

Sweep the net through the water,

then tip your catch into a jar.

Now take a look.

Newts or fish?

Beetles? A squishy mass of eggs?

Wiggly worms or things with lots of legs?

Maybe you can figure out what they are

or maybe not.

The best thing about pond dipping

is just looking.

And when you're done—gently pour them back.

Tide Pooling

Along the beach are pools the sea has left behind,
caught between the rocks or scooped in sand.

There are wide pools, where the weeds wave like a forest
and small fish swim like flocks of birds.

There are deep pools, with dark ravines and canyons
where the fiercest crabs can hide and snap their claws.

There are pools all filled with sunlight
and the sudden sparkle of backward-swimming shrimp.

Each pool is a little world all of its own,
and you can be the first person to discover it.

Shell Song

Fans and cones and spirals
lying in the sand,
white and pink and yellow
in my hand.

Pyramids and angel's wings
lying in the sand,
pearly cream and midnight black
in my hand.

Bishop's hats and triton's horns
lying in the sand,
needle sharp and mirror smooth
in my hand.

Tide

Slowly, slowly the tide creeps in.
It trickles into rock pools,
nibbles at your sand castle,
then washes it away.

At last the bay is full of sea,
like a brimming cup.
And all the beach is underwater,
in another world,
until tomorrow.

Lizard

Quick as a blink!
What was it?
Fast as thinking—
there, then not there.
Quick as a blink.

Quick as a blink!
Eyes glinting,
tail whipping,
tongue flicking.

It's a lizard!
Quick as a blink.

Night

The breeze shivers through the barley,
and the sea sighs.

Far away an owl is calling
and a star shines.

The moon sails white and silver
in the dark sky.

Sometimes you can feel,
sometimes you can feel,
sometimes you can feel the world is turning.

FIVE REASONS TO KEEP CHICKENS

1. They look very silly when they are taking a dust bath.

2. They perch in the funniest places.

3. They will eat the caterpillars on your vegetables and chase flies (which is very funny).

4. The rooster looks so sweet when he sleeps with his wings around his hens.

5. Collecting eggs from under a hen when they are still warm is wonderful.

Moth

Phuttt! Phutttt!

Something's battering the lightbulb,

fluttering and fussing.

It has wings just like a butterfly,

but when it rests,

it folds them flat across its back.

It's a moth.

It flies at night

and steers by the moon's glow.

It got confused by the lamplight,

so it flew indoors.

Turn off the light

and leave the window open.

It will fly off, safe, into the dark.

Growing

The balcony's a jungle, full of plants,
growing food for all the neighbors!

Basil to go on Mr. Scarlatti's pizzas,
cilantro for Mrs. Singh's curries,
mint for Mom's tea when she gets home from work,
lettuce for Dad's sandwiches,

and tomatoes for everyone!

Dens

Dens are not like houses or tents.

Dens are a part of the outside,

and when you make one—using twigs, dead leaves,

bales of straw, or anything else you can pile up to

make walls around you—you are part of outside too.

Things to Do in Your Den

1. Sit and think.

2. Notice things, like the smell of the earth or what beetles are doing.

3. Get very close to birds and animals. You can see them,

but they can't see you.

4. Have adventures—your den can be anything you want it to be.

Autumn

Autumn is exciting! Trees turn flame colored,
and the wind makes a whirligig of fiery leaves.
Birds feast on berries, and the first frosts
sprinkle spiders' webs with
diamonds.

Wind

What drives the storm clouds over the sky?

What bends the trees and breaks their branches?

What snatches your hat and makes your coat flap?

What ripples the pond and ruffles the grass?

What brushes your cheek, soft as a kiss?

Whisper it—wind, wind, wind!

Leaves

Under people's feet on paths and sidewalks, floating on the pond,

leaves are everywhere, in mounds and drifts so deep you can wade through them.

Kick swirls of red and yellow, brown and orange into the frosty air.

GEESE

High up, above the roads and the houses,
geese are flying.
They make a wobbly arrow in the sky.

They're going somewhere warmer,
and when they're gone,
you know that winter's on its way.

Spiderlings

What left this sea of silver

that shines and shakes,

as if the breeze was ruffling the surface of a lake?

It's simply spider silk—

a million tiny strings,

the silken parachutes of baby spiderlings.

Feather

I found a feather on the ground.
It looked so sad and scruffy,
split into little spiky barbs.

I pulled it tight between my fingers,
the way a bird does with its beak;
the stringy barbs zipped back together,
to make the feather whole again.

Then I swooshed it through the air,
and I could feel it trying to fly!

ACORN

You must be patient if you plant an acorn
and wait to see the first green shoot, the tiny leaf.
Then it will grow, but slowly, slowly, slowly,
so slowly you will hardly notice it;
by the time you're grown up, it will still be small.

For the tree, the years pass by as quick as thinking,
but for you, the years are slow and hold a life.
When you come back,
you'll find the tree is still a youngster,
just big enough to give a little shade.
You'll hold your grandchild's hand and say,
"You must be patient if you plant an acorn."

Worms

Sometimes, in the rain and dark,
worms come up from underground.
They seem too small to be important,
but watch . . . the worms are recycling.

They pull dead leaves into their burrows for a feast,
then poop them out in tiny heaps called casts
that turn into a covering of rich new soil.

Without worms, there'd be no soil for plants to grow in,
there'd be no food for animals—or us—to eat.
So in the rain and dark, when worms come up
from underground, say "thank you" very quietly,
for the work they do.

Apples

Fresh from the tree,
the apple sits in your hand,
cool and round,
and streaked with sunset colors.

All around you in the orchard
there are other apples.
Apples grown for juice:
Jonathans and Ida Reds.

GRAVENSTEIN

Apples grown for cider: Gravensteins
and Tolman Sweets.

Apples grown for pies:
Ginger Golds and Northern Spies.

But the apple in your hand was grown for eating:
Walter Pease or Milo Gibson,
Honey Crisp or McIntosh.
Bite into its crisp, white flesh
and taste the sweetness.

JONATHAN

HONEY CRISP

Squirrel

Squirrel's going on a nut hunt:
down the tall tree,
across the wide lawn,
up the slippery pole,
along the wobbly wire.
Yum! Nuts!

Oh, no! The gardener's coming!
Quick! Quick! Quick!

74

Along the wire,
down the pole,
across the lawn,
up, up, up, up, into the tree.
Safe!

Fungi

Pale balls and spotted saucers up on stalks,
rubbery Frisbees on trunks of trees,
gray furry fuzz on fallen leaves,
skinny orange fingers poking through the grass.

They're not animals, and they're not plants.
They're something else—
they're fungi: toadstools, mushrooms, molds.

They've been here all along,
their string-like bodies
hidden in the soil, under bark, inside branches.

The wet weather's brought them out in these weird shapes,
and when they've spread their seeds, as fine as dust,
they'll disappear as quietly as they came.

The Loaf That Jack Baked

This is the loaf that Jack baked,
warm from the oven.

This is the flour, all fine and white,
that was mixed in the bowl
to make the loaf that Jack baked.

This is the ear of wheat, all gold,
that yielded the grain
that was ground to flour
to make the loaf that Jack baked.

This is the leaf and stalk, so green,
that grew the ear that yielded the grain
that was ground to flour
to make the loaf that Jack baked.

This is the seed, all round and ripe,
that sprouted the stalk that grew the ear
that yielded the grain that was ground to flour
to make the loaf that Jack baked.

This is the man, so straight and strong,
who sowed the seed that sprouted the stalk
that grew the ear that yielded the grain
that was ground to flour
to make the loaf that Jack baked.

It's warm from the oven.
Eat up!

Harvest

The garden has been busy,

growing squash, beans, and eggplants,

tomatoes, carrots, peas.

The tiny seeds planted in the spring

have used the sun and rain and soil to make all this!

And now it's time for harvest—

picking and pulling,

washing and chopping,

cooking, bottling, and freezing,

so that deep in winter there'll be

summer food to eat!

Berry Picking

Let's go berry picking!

Up the path, over the fence . . .

At first your basket seems too big, and then

not big enough, for berry picking.

Back home, we make a great, big pie

to share our berry picking.

Ask an adult to help you make a delicious berry crumble!

5½ cups berries (blackberries,
   blueberries, raspberries, or a mixture)

¾ cup sugar

2 tablespoons water

1½ cups flour

a pinch of salt

⅓ cup butter

⅓ cup sugar

Preheat oven to 350°F.

Wash the berries. Put them in an ovenproof dish layer by layer,
sprinkling some of the ¾ cup sugar over each layer. Add the water.
Measure the flour into a bowl, and mix in the salt.
Cut the butter into small pieces, and mix it into the flour.
Rub the butter and flour together until the mixture
looks like bread crumbs. Mix in the ⅓ cup sugar.

Spread the crumble mixture over the berries so they
are covered. Put the pan in the oven and bake for
45 minutes, until the crumble is golden brown.

Eat. Yum.

Winter

Winter is a slow, low time. Everything is hiding from the cold; just staying alive is enough. Days are short, but the long frosty nights blaze with stars and spring is just a moon or two away.

WINTER TREES

Winter trees are naked.
All their leaves are gone.
You can see their trunks,
some smooth and straight,
some bent and wrinkled.
You can see the way
some branches
dip down to the ground
and some reach up high.
And you can see
the crisscross patterns
that the twigs make
against the sky.

Starlings

So many little birds flying altogether—
    hundreds, thousands maybe,
        making waves and arcs and spirals in the sunset sky.

They look like smoke, or a curtain rippling in the breeze.
    Every turn and swoop they make together—
        as if their flying is a dance that they all know by heart.

All at once, it's their bedtime.
    Down they fly, a fat, dark rope of birds,
        disappearing downward to their roost.

THE HORSE

The horse is so big!
It runs across the field, mane flying.
It's exciting and scary at the same time.

But its warm breath smells of the barn,
of hay and comfort,
and when it takes the carrot from your hand,
its dark eye is quiet
and its nose is velvet,
softer than your own cheek.

90

Snow Song

Outside, the flakes swirl down out of the darkness,
turning blackest night to palest gray.
Listen, and you can hear the quiet,
as if every sound had been wrapped up and put away.

In the morning, you'll find the snow has kept a diary
of things that happened when you were asleep.
The animals and birds who ran about the garden
have left a snowy record of their feet.

Snow has covered up the dirt and clutter;
it's made the world look new and neat and clean.
You forget the other seasons and their colors;
for now, white seems more
beautiful than green.

Patchwork Pigeons

Patchwork pigeons, made of sky,
catch the rain clouds when they fly.

DEER IN THE DAWN

You didn't expect to see each other,
you and the deer.
You're both caught,
one foot off the ground, breath held,
both with hearts pounding.
The deer looks at you,
trying to decide what you might do.

You want to look at the deer—
so beautiful, so unexpected in the dawn—
but the deer is frightened,
and it leaps away.

It's gone.
You breathe again
and wonder if you dreamed it.

Just Ducks

The moment they think you're going to feed them,

the ducks come hurrying across the pond,

as if you'd pulled them by a string.

First two or three, then ten, then even more!

There are drakes, the boy ducks, with the brightest colors,

and girl ducks, with their quiet streaks of brown.

There are ducks that like to dive and those that dabble.

All of them, together, feasting, squabbling,

splashing silver drops of water on their feathery backs.

THE
STARS SHOW

One, by one, by one, by one,

the stars show,

making pinprick patterns in the night.

The stars are suns,

just like our own sun,

but very, very, very far away.

One, by one, by one, by one,

the sky fills with stars,

so many that you'd never count them.

BEACHCOMBING

Seaweed streamers, seagull bones, and

urchin shells, chipped and white as china cups.

Shingle jewels in blue and green that were once bits of broken bottle.

A can with funny writing from a country half a world away.

A single shoe, a plastic star,

old, old wood, so worn and gray it could be

from a pirate galleon.

A giant rope, thicker than your leg,

and a line of pink shells in a perfect row.

Seed Saving

You don't always need to buy seeds to grow vegetables. You can save your own seeds from one year to grow vegetables the next.

Almost any vegetable will flower and make seeds if you leave it to do its own thing, but the easiest seeds to save come from vegetables like pumpkins, squash, and beans.

Save bean seeds by leaving a few bean pods on the plant to ripen. Wait until they're hard and dry, then take out the beans.

Take out pumpkin seeds before you cook the pumpkin. Wash them, dry them on paper towels, then spread them out on newspaper in a cool, dry place until they are absolutely dry and quite hard.

When your seeds are dry, they're ready to be stored. Put them in little paper bags or envelopes. Don't put more than ten or fifteen seeds in one bag, so if one rots, it won't spread to all the others. Write the name of the seeds on the bag, and then store them somewhere cool, dry, and dark until it's time to plant them in the spring.

Sunflower Seeds

Pumpkin
SEEDS

A Bird Feast

Little birds look fatter on a frosty day, but underneath their fluffed-up feathers, they are skinny. Small birds get very hungry in cold weather, so why not give them a feast?

Bird Cakes

Ask an adult to help you gently melt some fat (lard or suet) in a pan. Mix in some unsalted seeds and nuts, cookie crumbs, stale cake, or bread. Pour the mixture into empty containers—old yogurt cups work well. Push a long piece of string down into each cupful. Leave the cakes to cool and set, take them out of the cups, then hang them by their strings where the birds can get them.

Add to your feast by putting out nuts and seeds on a bird table, but make sure it's safe from cats and dogs. And don't forget water—birds need clean water to drink and take a bath in. Then wait. Don't worry if the birds don't come at once; it may take a while for them to find your offerings.

But then . . . you'll

have a storm of wings outside your window.

First U.S. edition 2012

Library of Congress Cataloging-in-Publication Data is available.

Library of Congress Catalog Card Number 2011046637

ISBN 978-0-7636-5549-5

19 20 21 22 APS 14 13

Printed in Humen, Dongguan, China

This book was typeset in Clarendon.
The illustrations were done in mixed media.

Candlewick Press
99 Dover Street
Somerville, Massachusetts 02144

visit us at www.candlewick.com